Make Change Your Family Business Tradition

A FAMILY ——
BUSINESS
PUBLICATION

Family Business Publications are the combined efforts of the Family Business Consulting Group and Palgrave Macmillan. These books provide useful information on a broad range of topics that concern the family business enterprise, including succession planning, communication, strategy and growth, family leadership, and more. The books are written by experts with combined experiences of over a century in the field of family enterprise and who have consulted with thousands of enterprising families the world over, giving the reader practical, effective, and time-tested insights to everyone involved in a family business.

, founded in 1994, is the leading business consultancy exclusively devoted to helping family enterprises prosper across generations.

FAMILY BUSINESS LEADERSHIP SERIES

This series of books comprises concise guides and thoughtful compendiums to the most pressing issues that anyone involved in a family firm may face. Each volume covers a different topic area and provides the answers to some of the most common and challenging questions.

Titles include:

Developing Family Business Policies: Your Guide to the Future
Effective Leadership in the Family Business
Family Business Compensation
Family Business Governance: Maximizing Family and Business Potential
Family Business Ownership: How to Be an Effective Shareholder
Family Business Succession: The Final Test of Greatness
Family Business Values: How to Assure a Legacy of Continuity and Success
The Family Constitution: Agreements to Secure and Perpetuate Your Family and Your Business
Family Education for Business-Owning Families: Strengthening Bonds by Learning Together
Family Meetings: How to Build a Stronger Family and a Stronger Business
Financing Transitions: Managing Capital and Liquidity in the Family Business
From Siblings to Cousins: Prospering in the Third Generation and Beyond
How Families Work Together
How to Choose and Use Advisors: Getting the Best Professional Family Business Advice
Working for a Family Business: A Non-Family Employee's Guide to Success
Letting Go: Preparing Yourself to Relinquish Control of the Family Business
Make Change Your Family Business Tradition
Making Sibling Teams Work: The Next Generation
More than Family: Non-Family Executives in the Family Business
Nurturing the Talent to Nurture the Legacy: Career Development in the Family Business
Preparing Successors for Leadership: Another Kind of Hero
Preparing Your Family Business for Strategic Change

All of the books were written by members of the Family Business Consulting Group and are based on both our experiences with thousands of client families as well as our empirical research at leading research universities the world over.

Make Change Your Family Business Tradition

Craig E. Aronoff
and John L. Ward

palgrave
macmillan

First published by the Family Business Consulting Group Publications, 2010.

This edition first published in 2011 by
PALGRAVE MACMILLAN®
in the United States—a division of St. Martin's Press LLC,
175 Fifth Avenue, New York, NY 10010.

Where this book is distributed in the UK, Europe and the rest of the world, this is by Palgrave Macmillan, a division of Macmillan Publishers Limited, registered in England, company number 785998, of Houndmills, Basingstoke, Hampshire RG21 6XS.

Palgrave Macmillan is the global academic imprint of the above companies and has companies and representatives throughout the world.

Palgrave® and Macmillan® are registered trademarks in the United States, the United Kingdom, Europe and other countries.

ISBN 978-0-230-11112-7   ISBN 978-0-230-11614-6 (eBook)
DOI 10.1057/9780230116146

Library of Congress Cataloging-in-Publication Data

Aronoff, Craig E.
    Make change your family business tradition / by Craig E. Aronoff and John L. Ward.
        p. cm. —(Family business leadership series)
    Originally published: Marietta, GA : Family Enterprise Publishers, c2001.
        Includes index.

        1. Family-owned business enterprises—Management. 2. Small business—Management. I. Ward, John L., 1945– II. Title.

HD62.25.A7646 2011
658.4'06—dc22   2010045295

A catalogue record of the book is available from the British Library.

Design by Newgen Imaging Systems (P) Ltd., Chennai, India.

First Palgrave Macmillan edition: January 2011

10 9 8 7 6 5 4 3 2 1

Contents

EXHIBITS vii

1 Introduction: The Challenge of Continuous Renewal . . 1

2 Change in a Family Business: How Hard Can It Be? . . . 9

3 Building and Preserving a Foundation for Change 19

4 Where Change Comes From 33

5 Leading Change in a Family Firm:
   A Guide for the Successor 39

6 Managing Resources for Change. 59

7 A Word to the Outgoing CEO 67

8 Creating a Tradition of Change 73

9 Summary .79

INDEX. 83

THE AUTHORS 91

Exhibits

Exhibit 1
Change in a Family Business: Easy or Hard? 15

Exhibit 2
Inhibitors to Change 17

Exhibit 3
Change that Protects the Heart of Your Business 28

Exhibit 4
Reinterpreting Values for Contemporary Challenges 30

Exhibit 5
A Leader's Model for Creating Change 51

Exhibit 6
Desirable Characteristics of Change Leaders 57

Exhibit 7
Building Blocks of Change in a Family Firm 61

Exhibit 8
Ideal Incumbents 69

Exhibit 9
Five Ways to Keep Your Strategy Fresh 74

Exhibit 10
Change Is Easier When You... 78

Chapter 1

Introduction

The Challenge of Continuous Renewal

Since its inception in 1992, a newsletter that we publish, the *Family Business Advisor*, has frequently included a feature called "Century of Success," which tells the stories of family businesses that have lasted more than 100 years. One of the most constant themes that emerges from these stories is this: **Family businesses that endure over a long period of time are those that do not just learn to respond to and adapt to a changing environment. They also learn to take the initiative and create change,** as necessary, in anticipation of what they expect to take place in the world around them. The ability to be resilient in the face of change and the ability to initiate change within the organization itself have enabled these business families to overcome setbacks and thrive. These are families that recognize how vital change is to ongoing success.

We mean it when we say these families *learn* both to respond to change and to create it. In their early years, not even the most enduring family businesses necessarily understand the importance of change. Consider the Bissell family in Grand Rapids, Michigan, for example. Melville Bissell invented the famous Bissell carpet sweeper in 1876, and he and his wife, Anna, created a company, BISSELL, Inc., that has lasted to this day.

But before 1952, when the founders' grandson, the third M. R. "Mel" Bissell, took over, the company was stagnating. Sales had reached about $5 million at the turn of the century and stayed there for over 50 years. The company was marked by paternalism, little innovation in products or marketing, and a dedication to providing family members with job security. Over a period of five years, Mel Bissell introduced vacuum cleaners, carpet shampooers, and other products. A new controller and a new data processing system enhanced management, and outside advertising and public-relations agencies beefed up marketing. Mel hired able non-family executives and expanded production. Annual sales had grown to $25 million by 1970, when Mel turned leadership of the company over to his cousin, John M. Bissell.

Family businesses that endure over a long period of time are those that do not just learn to respond to and adapt to a changing environment.
They also learn to take the initiative and create change, as necessary, in anticipation of what they expect to take place in the world around them.

John continued to initiate change. Much to the shock of family members, John, with Mel's support, encouraged some family executives to leave the company to make way for more competent non-family executives. Policies were established to set standards for the entry of family members into the business. Under John's leadership, the company grew to more than 3,000 employees and annual sales exceeding $400 million. John retired at age 65, becoming chairman of BISSELL and setting the stage for even more change.

If you are the leader of a family business or
expect to assume leadership in the near future,
your number-one challenge: preserving the best
of the past while creating a company that is able
not only to accept but to initiate changes.

By daring to break from tradition, Mel and John Bissell
helped assure the continued success of the firm their grandparents founded. They paved the way for BISSELL, Inc., to become
a diversified, international corporation. In so doing, they made
change a way of business life. At the same time, they respected
the past. As John once put it, BISSELL **"keeps the best of the
old but stays vibrant and growing by remaining open to new
ideas."**

Recognition of the need for change did not come intuitively
to BISSELL, Inc. It took vision to see the need and required skill-
ful leadership to help the organization institutionalize change as
part of an ongoing business strategy.

This book is about helping you and your family business do
what BISSELL and other enduring, successful family businesses
have done: **make change your tradition. If you are the leader
of a family business or expect to assume leadership in the near
future,** this book will help you manage what we think is **your
number-one challenge: preserving the best of the past while
creating a company that is able not only to accept but to initiate changes** that enhance business and family adaptability, sus-
tainability, and success. You will learn how leading change in a
family business is different from leading change in a non-family
corporation, and you will be shown skill-building ideas and tech-
niques for creating and responding to change. This book will
also help you think about change and how to use it so that your

business can grow and succeed. And it will help you manage change that is thrust upon you.

If you are a CEO nearing the time of generational transition, this book will give you a new appreciation of the importance of change and show you how you can support your successors as they move to initiate changes to advance your company. When John Bissell determined that certain family executives needed to be eased out of the business, former CEO Mel Bissell supported him by taking charge of the actual terminations. Consequently, ensuing ill will was aimed at Mel, not the new CEO. While we would hope that your support of a successor would not have to be so drastic or controversial, the Bissells offer an excellent example of the concept.

If you are a non-family executive and a successor is taking over, you may feel particularly vulnerable. You have given many years of service to the company and much loyalty to the senior generation. Now new leadership means change, and you may feel threatened, wondering how the changes will affect you. It is our hope that this book will offer insights that help you contribute to change rather than becoming change's victim.

Perhaps you are a member of the board of directors of a family business. If so, you play a crucial role as an advocate for continued business success. Your insights on matters of business and your understanding relationship with family owners can be important elements of the change process. This book should help you understand more fully how change relates specifically to a *family* business and increase your value as a board member in supporting change.

Or perhaps you are a member of a business-owning family but are not involved in the day-to-day operations of the business. Still, you may care deeply about it and what the business means to the family in terms of legacy, relationships, community standing, and financial well-being. It is our hope that this book will help you understand the necessity for change in the business—and the risk that accompanies change—so that you can offer encouragement to family members who are actively managing the company. They will need your support in making appropriate changes, but they can also use your ideas about how to lead change while preserving the valuable heritage of your family's business.

Sometimes the issues surrounding change are confused with succession issues. The senior-generation CEO may be seen by the next-generation successor as resistant to new ideas or new risks and as unwilling to let go. At the same time, the successor may be viewed by the CEO as too hasty to make changes or as insensitive to what the business stands for in the family and in the community. A struggle ensues. A CEO already reluctant to pass on a life's work to the next generation may dig his heels in even harder.

But change is a given. It is a fact of life. Industries are consolidating. The marketplace is becoming more global and increasingly electronic. Product life cycles are becoming shorter and shorter. Competition is intensifying. And the pace of change is ever accelerating.

The world that today's senior generation grew up in offered a considerably different business climate than we are experiencing now. **From the beginning of the Industrial Revolution until as late as the 1970s, the prevailing view of business was that you found a need, developed a product or service to meet the need, and protected your niche by consistently improving your product or service. Management focused on control and assuring consistency. Typically, the proprietor's oldest son was expected to sit at his father's elbow, watching** and learning how he did things and then do them the way Dad did.

But this is the post-industrial era, or in more popular parlance, the Information Age or the New Economy. **Rapid change quickly depreciates the value of everyone's knowledge. While the older generation has valuable lessons to offer the younger generation, one doesn't learn to lead a dynamic business at anyone's elbow.** After young potential leaders have left home for education and experience and to gain a broader perspective, a battle with their parents over the need for change in the company is not an unusual occurrence.

Rapid change quickly depreciates the value of everyone's knowledge. While the older generation has valuable lessons to offer the younger generation, one doesn't learn to lead a dynamic business at anyone's elbow.

In the past, it was possible for a family business leader to build one strategic success and make it last for the 20 or 25 years of his or her tenure. That is no longer possible, and therein lies a major challenge: **today's family business leaders, if they lead for a generation, must lead an organization that has two, three, or four waves of strategic renewal during their tenures.** In other words, the leader of a family business typically will stay in place for more than 20 years, but the business's strategy now has to change several times during the course of those two decades.

More than ever before, family businesses must be prepared to reinvent themselves to meet the demands of rapid change and evolving competition. As organizations, they must be innovative, adaptive, and flexible. Management today means effectively managing change, and that is the primary responsibility of the successor CEO.

This book will help you make a distinction between change issues and succession issues. More important, we hope it will serve your company as a tool in the process of change and help you incorporate change as a company tradition. We encourage you to share this book with all the key players in your company so that they can join the crucial process of making change your tradition.

Chapter 2

Change in a Family Business

How Hard Can It Be?

Accepted wisdom suggests that family businesses are more flexible, more innovative, and more responsive to market changes than publicly held companies. Family firms don't have to answer to outside shareholders. They can move quickly. They can turn on a dime.

But having the potential to move quickly and actually doing it can be another matter entirely.

When it comes to change, family businesses present a paradox: **in some ways, it is easier to change a family business; in other ways, it is much more difficult.**

Family businesses are more suited to change for a number of reasons. Owners can make decisions quickly, if they so choose. They don't have to play politics, fighting their way through a maze of bureaucrats to get action. They should be able to withstand the dissatisfactions that occur with change because they are the owners and their jobs are secure. And in a good working environment, non-family employees will trust the owners' decisions and not fear for their jobs.

On the whole, family firms are smaller and more entrepreneurial. The owner of a family firm can influence the business's culture more quickly and more pervasively than can the leaders of large, unwieldy organizations.

Despite the existence of assets like these that support the ability to change, we believe that the process of change in a family business is not only different but can be much more difficult.

IMPEDIMENTS TO CHANGE

To establish the conditions for creating a culture of change, family business leaders must understand just what makes change so hard in a family firm. Here are some of the impediments to change that characterize family-owned companies. As you consider them, you will see that some of these obstacles are also the very strengths that make a family business successful, which makes change an even more complicated affair:

♦ **Longer tenure of CEOs and other top leaders.** While the leader of a non-family company may be CEO for an average of six or seven years, the leader of a family firm may run the show for a whole generation. Long tenures offer advantages. Mature family firms with long-tenured key executives understand the cycles in their industries and have learned how to cope with downturns. They can resist short-term temptations—such as overcommitting to growth in boom times—and take the long view.

But unless a leader has created a culture of change, little innovation may have taken place beyond that which the CEO introduced during his or her first few years of being in charge. The same can be said of other key leaders. While longer top executive tenures can create stability in family firms, stagnation can also result.

Researchers have found that CEOs too long in the job become set in their ways and views, no longer grow in knowledge, and are increasingly unmotivated and out of touch. They become bored and fatigued, not because they are too old but because of the length of time in their position. Two characteristics we frequently find in successful family firms are a mandatory retirement date and a conscientious effort by the CEO to be accountable to others who challenge the currency of his of her thinking.

"Replace your leadership every ten years," advises Roy Richards Jr., the second-generation chairman and CEO of Carrollton, Georgia–based Southwire Corp., one of the largest manufacturers of power cables in the world. Change is happening so fast—workers are different, consumers are different—that he says, "I believe in temporary leadership. There are presidents and CEOs who can lead a business through 20 or 30 years of success, but I think that is rare. You've got to always keep fresh leadership in the business who, hopefully, are family members. Continuous fresh leadership is critical."

♦ **Love, respect, and loyalty.** Typically, the successor to the chief executive in a family business is the son or daughter of that chief executive. The CEO is both the parent and the mentor of the heir apparent. Not wishing to appear unloving, disrespectful, or disloyal, members of the next generation may be reluctant to push for change. Or if they do, they may be seen by the parent/CEO as "wet behind the ears" or as naively spouting theories they learned in business school. In some cases, the parent may feel a sense of betrayal and be suspicious that the son or daughter who initiates change is trying to push the parent out.

In short, successors-to-be are required by the demands of competition to be champions of change at a time when they are still naturally subordinate and still lack credibility in the face of highly credible, powerful people whom they love and whose approval is very important to them. No wonder change is so difficult!

◆ **Tradition and past success.** When tradition becomes "the way we've always done things around here," without a genuine examination of what a company's current values and practices are or should be, tradition acts as a leash. It holds a company back. When certain practices and ways of doing things have made a company successful, there's a temptation to continue doing things the same way. Family members may be inclined to say, "Why wreck a good thing?" Or, "If it ain't broke, don't fix it." But if your business continues to do things in the same way, those traditional practices may keep it from being successful in the future. The lure of doing things "the way we've always done them" may prohibit family managers and key non-family employees from anticipating the need for change. Such a danger helped give rise to the popular newer mandate, "If it ain't broke, break it!"

The strategy that made your company successful during the past generation is unlikely to keep it successful for the next generation.

Success not only leads to the institutionalization of traditions that may, over time, prove ineffectual, it also leads to complacency. If yours is a healthy family business, you may believe that the way to stay healthy is to keep on doing what you're doing. **But the strategy that made your company successful during the past generation is unlikely to keep it successful for the next generation.**

The hardest time to make changes is when things are fine. Why, you may wonder, should you put yourself through all the stress and risk and ambiguity of making changes when things are going so well? Keep in mind that it's easy to accuse others of "fearing" change when they seem resistant to it. But in our view, **complacency is also a way of resisting change and is a greater enemy of change than fear.**

♦ **Hero worship.** When a company has been run by a powerful, charismatic leader, family members and non-family members alike tend to want to remain loyal to that leader's vision or way of doing things, despite a need for change. At one major family-controlled firm, the third-generation CEO's challenge in following a heroic predecessor was symbolized by the fact that his father was known as "John God" while he was called "John Boy." When a CEO is so revered, changing strategies and practices that he or she put into place is particularly difficult for a successor. But when business conditions required it, "John Boy" made such changes and his father supported him.

♦ **Family culture.** A family business's culture usually grows out of the values and beliefs of the founding family. Family members who are not involved in the daily operation of the business, in an effort to remain consistent to what they believe are family values, resist change in the business. They identify the business with the past—with the parent-founder and with the family. They confuse their love for the parent-founder with the values and practices in the business. When the successor recognizes the need for change in the business and tries to initiate it, non-active family members view such efforts as a threat to their identity. They ask, "What's she doing—rebelling against our father?" Or, "Is our brother on some kind of ego trip?" Or, "Why is he taking away something that was so good?" Thus the successor is not trusted if he or she sees the need for change. Even brothers and sisters may be resistant to change as a result of lingering sibling rivalry.

A different problem altogether occurs when successors are so steeped in family culture that they cannot see the need for change. For example, when a son embraces the past with great devotion, as expected in some cultures or societies, he will not be able to see the necessity of change or the way to change.

♦ **Key non-family employees.** Non-family executives may be fearful of what a change in leadership will mean. They have been loyal for a long time to the outgoing CEO and may be just as loyal to his or her policies and practices. Like inactive family members, they may see change as signs of disrespect or rebellion. Even more, they may be concerned about retaining their jobs.

When these impediments are coupled with a family firm's tendency to insulate itself from change, creating change becomes even harder. Take a business in a protected niche, for example, and suppose its founder has instituted a no-debt policy that is still observed. Instead of creating an environment in which change can be stimulated, the leaders of such a business will do everything they can to insulate themselves against threat, risk, and change. They are complacent because, so far, their niche is safe. And, honoring the family tradition, they will not take on debt. As a result, the company becomes paralyzed and cannot grow. And when someone else discovers the niche and begins to move in, the insular company ends up being especially vulnerable.

Ideally, the incumbent CEO has created a culture of change in the family business, setting the stage for a successor to continue the tradition of leading change. If this is not the case, the successor must take on the challenge of initiating

---

EXHIBIT 1   Change in a Family Business: Easy or Hard?

Reasons change is **easier** in a family business than a public company:

- Smaller and more entrepreneurial than most public companies
- Ability to move quickly—less bureaucracy, fewer decision makers
- Few or no outside shareholders
- Less dissatisfaction with change because owners' jobs are secure
- Owners have more influence on company culture

Reasons change is **harder**:

- Longer tenures of CEOs—may lead to stagnation
- Fear of seeming disloyal to incumbent or outgoing CEO if you change things
- Tradition and past success—the attitude of "Why change when we've been so successful?"
- Family culture may be resistant to business change
- Family members' anxiety over financial security
- Everyone has grown up in the same culture, so it's difficult to see things differently

change in a resistant culture and establishing change as a new tradition.

It works better when the incumbent/outgoing CEO supports change. Frieda Caplan, the founder of Frieda's, Inc., a nationally known Los Angeles–based produce importer, turned the reins of the business over to her daughter, Karen Caplan, in 1986. Frieda recalls that as her first presidential action, Karen wanted to send a message industrywide letting everyone know there would be no changes in operation. Frieda countered: "Are you crazy? Of course there are going to be changes. This is not a nominal title I'm giving you." To give Karen the opportunity to start making those changes, Frieda left town for her first vacation in 25 years.

Karen implemented professional management systems, developed departments, wrote a mission statement, and launched a total quality management program. In the first seven years under her leadership, the company's sales grew from $10 million to $22.5 million, and the staff grew from 54 to 110—a testament to her mother's belief that Karen would make the right changes.

> Ideally, the incumbent CEO has created a culture of change in the family business, setting the stage for a successor to continue the tradition of leading change.

EXHIBIT 2 Inhibitors to Change

When surveyed, a large group of family firms identified the following as the major inhibitors to business change:

1. Longtime loyalty to key managers and key advisors . 25%
2. Risk averseness of family leaders 18%
3. Deeply entrenched traditions 14%
4. Insulation from outside world by family leaders . . 14%
5. Inertia of success 10%
6. Paternalistic management style of family leaders . . 10%
7. Long tenures of leadership by family business leader . . 8%

Chapter 3

Building and Preserving a Foundation for Change

One business theory holds that to lead change, the successor must attack past memories and myths. Psychiatrist Abraham Zaleznik of the Harvard Business School writes that leading change requires personal objectivity—"the ability to see the world as it is." Such objectivity enables the leader to reconceptualize the business's strategy while others around the leader may deny the need to change.

The more successful a business has been and the more intense its values, he suggests, the more past practices and past values will be reinforced. Ironically, it seems, **the greater the past success, the greater the resistance to change.**

"To transform individual objectivity into collective culture requires an act of symbolic patricide...killing the father, metaphorically speaking," writes Zaleznik in his book, *Learning Leadership* (Bonus Books, 1993). Otherwise, he argues, change is not possible. The organization will still warmly remember past successes and heroes and hang on to those comfortable feelings.

Effective change is rooted in a clearly understood
and frequently examined foundation of values.

We believe there is important food for thought in what
Zaleznik has to say. However, when it comes to family businesses, we believe the notion of overtly attacking the past is
one that needs to be set aside. What works for a non-family
organization may not necessarily be successfully applied to a
family firm.

While the ability to change is critical in any business, we
have learned that continuity, constancy, and tradition are among
the keys that help family firms to flourish. What we have found
in the long-lasting businesses that we have observed over the
years is that effective change is rooted in a clearly understood
and frequently examined foundation of values. We have also
found that successful business families understand the difference
between their values and their traditions.

A foundation of values, what one family calls
the "bedrock of values," provides the ongoing support that makes effective change possible and enables a business to cope with rapid
change.

What makes family businesses family businesses—what gives
them their competitive advantage and makes them strong—is
the fact that they're good at building, maintaining, and managing
a core culture of values. They pay attention to why things are
done, how people are treated, and the importance of relationships.

(For more information on values, please see the Family Business Leadership Series title *Family Business Values: How to Assure a Legacy of Continuity and Success.*) **A foundation of values, what one family calls the "bedrock of values," provides the ongoing support that makes effective change possible and enables a business to cope with rapid change.** Most of us are not built for the pace of change that we're experiencing in the world today. People need something steadfast to cling to—the solid footing that a core of values can provide. For this reason, we make the following recommendations:

• **Be evolutionary, not revolutionary.** Arie de Geus, the author of *The Living Company: Habits For Survival in a Turbulent Business Environment* (Harvard Business Press, 1997), suggests that a business has a heart around which all its resources, including people, organize themselves. Don't make change by ripping out the heart of your company.

• **Respect the past.** This does not mean that you don't make necessary changes—you must. What it does mean is that you honor what went before, while at the same time **consciously** re-affirming old values and adopting new ideas as appropriate, and reshaping traditions to meet today's realities.

• **Understand the difference between values and traditions.** Values are what you as a family and as a family business stand for. The *American Heritage Dictionary* describes a value as "a principle, standard, or quality considered worthwhile or desirable." **A tradition, passed down from generation to generation, is a custom that exemplifies a value. It is not the value itself.**

• **Find out what's already there.** Business families need to talk about and identify what values they hold—hard work, service, integrity, quality, loyalty, and so on. Once you understand what those core values are, you can reinterpret them and make them work for you in ways that are relevant to your contemporary challenges. And you will need to articulate them in such a way that will help everybody else understand them and "buy in." (For exercises that help you understand what values your family holds, please see the Family Business Leadership Series title *Family Business Values: How to Assure a Legacy of Continuity and Success*.)

THE DARK SIDE OF TRADITIONS

While traditions can be a source of strength to a family and its business, they have their dark side. They can be dangerous things. When they are observed slavishly or without thought given to their relevance for the present, traditions can put a company in a straitjacket. Here are some additional ways to think about values and traditions that illustrate how they differ:

• Values and beliefs represent WHY we do things. Tradition means WHAT we're doing, or HOW we're doing things.

• Tradition means "we do it this way because we've always done it this way." Values mean "we do it this way because it expresses our beliefs, reflects who we are, and contributes to the meaning of our lives."

• Values are iron, while tradition may be the rust that forms on its surface over a long period of time. To make sure your organization is functioning well, sometimes you have to remove the rust. (But don't remove the iron!)

Tradition is lethal to a company when it becomes rust. Certain practices may be adhered to in a family firm because they are the practices that made the business successful in the past. They may be practices, however, that will keep **the company from being successful in the future.**

When we think of culture as What we're doing and How we're doing it—for example, how we advertise, how we run meetings, how we pay the sales force—**we become inflexible to change.** All the things we used to do become synonymous with our traditions.

But **when we think of our company culture as** _Why_ **we do things, we can think in terms of values and beliefs. That view allows us to be flexible about our behavior and practices—that is, about How we do things.** If we value integrity, for example, whatever we do and however we do it, we're going to do it with integrity. If we value respect for people, whatever actions we take will demonstrate our respect for people.

The business family must separate the tradition from the value itself and ask whether the tradition or practice still successfully serves the value. **While you may want to hold on to the values of the past, you may find you need to discard the practices of the past.** The following examples should illustrate.

When we think of our company culture as _Why_ we do things, we can think in terms of values and beliefs. That view allows us to be flexible about our behavior and practices—that is, about How we do things.

THE NEYER FAMILY:
PRESERVING FUNDAMENTAL VALUES

More than 100 years old, Al. Neyer, Inc., is a fast-growing, fast-changing real estate company based in Cincinnati. In the late 1980s, it was a contracting company that did a little bit of real estate development. A decade later, it had been transformed into an increasingly sophisticated and complicated multidivisional business engaged in office, industrial, and retail development and construction; real estate management and ownership; and joint ventures with other firms. Sales in 1998 neared the $60 million mark, almost double what they were three years earlier.

However, the fifth-generation Neyers who now run the company say they have not forgotten their roots. They attribute the company's success and endurance to family core values that put the common good ahead of everything else.

The company dates back to 1894, when Joseph Neyer Sr. began as a carpentry contractor, building churches and schools. The company now bears the name of his grandson, Alphonse (Al), who added public works and occasional commercial projects to its mix. In 1963, after Al's three sons joined the business, Al. Neyer, Inc., purchased its first land for commercial development.

When the last of Al's sons retired in 1998, the departure was accompanied by an announcement of a restructuring with three major components:

1. The establishment of a formal board of directors that included, for the first time, members who were not family owners.
2. A senior management team that, for the first time, included executives who were not members of the owning group.

The company, says David F. Neyer, who was chosen by his fifth-generation cousins as president and CEO, "needed specific skill sets that were not represented within the Neyer family—namely, finance and accounting, architecture, and asset property management."

3. A family ownership group, a special vehicle that would enable owners to address ownership issues separately from issues they faced as managers and employees.

The objectives and responsibilities of each group were clearly spelled out on paper. Among the responsibilities assigned to the board, for example, is: "Measure company performance against core values and financial objectives established by Family Ownership Group."

Trust and mutual support—being concerned about what's best for the other members in the group—are the keys to the company's long-lived success, says William L. Neyer, vice president of the company's design-build operations. He traces those traits back to his grandparents, Al and Gertrude. During the Depression, he says, relating a family story, Al Neyer used to keep a box of money on his dresser. If his sons—Raymond A., Donald L., and Thomas L. Sr.—needed money, they could take it from the box. "But you didn't take it irresponsibly, and you were willing to explain why you needed it, if anybody asked," says Bill, "so my dad and his two brothers trusted each other's judgment."

The three brothers made decisions by consensus—the way the management group makes decisions today. Furthermore, says Bill, "They were committed to what makes sense for the business and for the Neyer family and not necessarily what makes sense for Ray Neyer or Tom Neyer or Don Neyer."

The family still has in its possession a document dated November 11, 1954, written in Al Neyer's own hand. He called it

"Rules of conduct in relations with Father and Sons associated in business." Its insistence on mutual respect still guides the family today.

"The family relationship should not allow degeneration of differences into quarrels," he admonished in one rule. "We differ with our friends but do not allow these differences to interfere with personal feelings."

In another rule, he seemed to be speaking to himself: "Fathers should call on their past experiences with others and accord to their sons at least as courteous treatment as is given to others."

Forty years later, in a letter to a local business newspaper, Al's son Tom said of his father: "As we continue to turn the operation of Al. Neyer, Inc., over to yet another generation, his wisdom becomes all the more evident."

At the beginning of the new millennium, the corporate vision was to become a full-service provider for anybody with

---

Al. Neyer, Inc., Core Values

- Follow the Golden Rule—treat others as you would like to be treated.
- Turn the other cheek—that is, do not abandon your business ethics even when others abandon theirs.
- Your family is your primary obligation.
- Honesty and integrity at all times with our customers, our suppliers, our business associates, ourselves, and with everyone.
- Remember always that you have an obligation to fully use your talents to better the world around you—i.e., be a "model for others."

a real estate need—anywhere in the country. The company mission statement used to speak of Al. Neyer, Inc., as "Greater Cincinnati's leading commercial real estate developer." But during a company strategic planning session, the reference to Cincinnati was removed, signaling the company's broader geographic ambitions.

"Our fathers don't have anything but pride about the direction in which we've gone," says Dave.

THE MYERS FAMILY: A COMMITMENT TO KIDS

Ever since the magazine *Highlights for Children* was first published in 1946, its motto has been the same: "Fun with a purpose." In addition, the Highlights Creed, developed by the magazine's founders, the husband-and-wife team of Dr. Garry Cleveland Myers and Caroline Clark Myers, still appears on the masthead:

> *This book of wholesome fun is dedicated to helping children grow in basic skills and knowledge, in creativeness, in ability to think and reason, in sensitivity to others, in high ideals, and worthy ways of living— for children are the world's most important people.*

This philosophy guides editorial and business decisions at the parent corporation, Highlights for Children, Inc. (HFC), with offices in Columbus, Ohio, and Honesdale, Pennsylvania. The family weighs every idea by the founders' acid test: what's that going to do for children? No article, marketing tactic, or new venture is likely to be pursued if it doesn't provide something positive for children.

EXHIBIT 3   Change that Protects the Heart of Your
Business
+ Is evolutionary, not revolutionary
+ Respects the past
+ Differentiates between values and traditions
+ Is based on core values but meets the needs of today and
  the future

That doesn't mean the company doesn't change when it needs to. It owes its success to family members who know what to change and what to preserve. HFC now has annual sales of more than $100 million and employs 700 people in such enterprises as children's book publishing, a periodical for elementary schoolteachers, and a firm that runs seminars and conferences for teachers and school administrators. In the 1990s alone, HFC created or acquired five additional divisions. It also has kept up with technology, producing CD-ROM products and launching its own website, which includes an online catalog.

"More change has been occurring than most people are aware of," CEO Garry Cleveland Myers III once told us. His cousin, *Highlights* editor Kent Brown, added: "I don't think we have any commitment to a MAGAZINE. We have a commitment to KIDS."

Everything at HFC is up for change except the company's core values and mission. But the company seeks to implement change subtly, to preserve the family business's image. Take a look at the company's website (www.highlightsforchildren.com) and you'll see the evidence. While HFC has jumped into the world of the Internet, there's the enduring motto on the home page: "Fun with a purpose."

SAVORING THE PAST, CHANGING FOR THE FUTURE

The challenge—perhaps the most difficult challenge facing successors as they seek to become successful leaders—is respecting traditions and the past while at the same time creating a culture of change. Two of our favorite examples of this concept have been one company whose motto is "Where change is our tradition," and another that emphasizes, "Tradition is not history; it is eternity." Both mottos stress that **successors need to develop an organizational climate eager to change without discarding or discrediting the strengths of the past.**

More recently, we became acquainted with a company from Brazil that put it best of all with the slogan: "New ideas, old ideals." That expression adds a new depth to our thinking. The goal, it seems, is to preserve the values of the past while assuring decision-making innovation and flexibility for the future. In family firms, the ideals of the past often include such values as integrity, trusted relationships, the highest standards, respect for people, and commitment to community. Such values are timeless. It's just the way they're practiced that may need to change in order to keep a family business fresh and competitive.

EXHIBIT 4 Reinterpreting Values for Contemporary Challenges

Original Value	Old Behavior/Tradition	Problem
1. We take care of family.	We employ any family member who wants a job.	Family members in it just for security hold the company back.
2. We take care of employees.	No one is laid off or fired.	The value becomes an unrealistic expectation.
3. We don't expose our company to financial risk.	Company takes on no debt.	Company's ability to grow is limited.
4. We go the extra mile.	Company does anything for anybody.	Approach is unprofitable, and family members exhaust themselves trying to meet expectations.
5. Since we're family, we ALL take care of everything.	Family members in the business take responsibility for everything.	Chaos results. Employees don't know which family member is responsible for what.
6. We celebrate and honor our people.	Employees are recognized for loyalty, tireless effort, and picking up the slack for somebody else.	There is stagnation of ideas, too little change in the company.

Reinterpreted Value	New Behavior/Tradition
We take care of family in or out of the business.	Buy out family members holding company back; they can invest the proceeds for income. Retain family members who want to grow the business and can contribute.
We take care of employees by enabling them to take care of themselves.	Provide training and help employees continuously develop their skills rather than continuously provide jobs.
We do not expose our company to inappropriate financial risk.	Company takes on debt in a conservative, disciplined manner in order to grow.
We go the extra mile for our best customers.	Company goes out of its way for customers with which it has profitable relationships.
We all care intensely about our business and pay careful attention to it.	Each family member has his or her own area of authority for which they are held accountable but may comment on other areas under appropriate circumstances (e.g., management meetings or board meetings).
We celebrate and honor our people.	Employees are recognized for creating new ideas or for empowering other people.

Chapter 4

Where Change Comes From

It's one of the facts of life: Nothing is constant except change. Let's look at some of the events—or changes—that trigger change within a family business:

◆ **Death, incapacitation, or retirement of a family member.** While the death of any company's CEO is always traumatic, in a family business, the death of family members—and non-family key executives—can have a profound effect as well. We talked about the Myers family of Highlights for Children, Inc., in the previous chapter. In the 1950s, the founders' son, Garry Cleveland Myers Jr. and his wife, Mary, masterminded new marketing strategies that led to long-term profitability for HFC. Garry Jr. helped to successfully run the company until he, Mary, and a non-family vice president were killed in a 1960 plane crash. A non-family president ran the company until members of the third generation were ready for leadership.

◆ **Changes in the economy, good or bad.** The U.S. economic boom of the late 1990s, for example, had a very strong impact on the home remodeling and home improvement industries. In some parts of the country, general contractors, house-painting companies, kitchen design firms, and electricians often had more work than they could handle. But smart business-owning families recognize that there will always be cycles and, even when times are good, prepare themselves—through diversification, for example—for the rough patches that will surely lie ahead. As one CEO, whose business had weathered many recessions, told us, "Your plan has to try to accommodate both ups and downs."

◆ **Shifts in your industry.** The introduction of the vacuum cleaner by competitors forced BISSELL, Inc., maker of the famous BISSELL carpet sweeper, to offer vacuum cleaners and other new products. Today, technological change is pushing many family firms to rethink the way they do business from top to bottom. In a three-generation business started by a young woman who brought in her mother and grandmother, the mother wanted to sell the company's products in a more traditional way, through direct mail. She ended up compromising with her daughter, agreeing to try the Internet and television as well.

◆ **Crises of almost any kind.** Years ago, S. Martinelli & Company, which made hard cider and fermented champagne cider, survived Prohibition because a young family member had developed the process for producing the first pasteurized, unfermented apple juice. This enabled the company to concentrate on the production of its non-alcoholic beverages. In 1989, Martinelli survived the Alar pesticide scare by immediately redeploying advertising dollars to inform consumers of the company's pesticide-free products.

Many other events can trigger change in a business. Declining performance or a missed dividend sends a quick message that changes need to be made. Marriages and divorces may affect the balance of power in the company or have an impact on its finances.

Barilla, a family-controlled Italian pasta maker founded in 1877, has managed to regenerate itself after episodes of war, soaring unemployment, and inflation. It even survived being owned by a large American corporation—with the financial help of a Swiss family business, the Barillas bought their company back after eight years of outside ownership. Barilla survived because of family members' resolve and because they responded to and initiated change—diversifying product lines when the opportunity arose, streamlining operations, and expanding internationally.

Obviously, changes can come from anywhere, at any time. Some changes can be anticipated so they don't take business owners quite so by surprise. For example, a company can and should develop disaster plans. Estate plans help a family business make the transition from one generation to the next. Buy–sell agreements help protect the financial health of a company from a variety of conflicts, and so on.

For many business owners, however, the rapid pace of change is exasperating. Too often we hear them say, "Business just isn't fun anymore!" They tell us that **their real problem is they feel they have less and less control over their own destiny** in this sea of roiling change. And that, they say, is what really gets to them.

Entrepreneurs, by their nature, their proven psychology, seek to control their own destiny. As one said, "All this change is tough enough, but so much of it is just irrational. How do I respond to it?"

We'd like to suggest fighting fire with fire, or, in this case, **meeting change with change.** If, as we encourage, you make change your tradition—if you **make it a policy to initiate change instead of just react to it**—we think you stand a better chance of feeling more in control of your own destiny.

While business owners need to respond nimbly and intelligently to change that is not of their own making, this book is more about **creating** change—strategic change that anticipates what will happen in the business environment and enables the family firm to survive and prosper. And like the change that happens *to* us, ideas for initiating change can come from anywhere. And that's a good thing.

What we mean by that is that new ideas are not solely the responsibility of the CEO. They can come from the younger generation as well as the senior generation. They can come from family members outside the business as well as those who are active in it. And new ideas often can and do come from employees, customers, your board of directors, and even suppliers.

One of the ways that the Seattle-based Laird Norton Company promotes change is by making it a point to cultivate widespread involvement of family members. Approaching 150 years old, this conglomerate of forest-related and other businesses enjoys annual sales exceeding $1 billion. Ownership is in the hands of more than 350 related individuals. While very few family members are involved in the actual business operations, there are places for family on company and subsidiary boards of directors, on standing and ad hoc committees, and in the family office, as well as other opportunities for contributing ideas and providing leadership.

In the late 1970s and early 1980s, Nathalie Simsak and a group of her fifth-generation cousins began to contact family members, inviting them to come up with ideas for both the family and the business. At a meeting in the early 1980s, one elder recalls, Nathalie encouraged her cousins to be brave and speak up.

In 1988, Nathalie became the company's first woman president. With the bulk of her experience in the volunteer sector, Nathalie had gained a wealth of insight from non-profit organizations that translated well into for-profit business.

During her administration, Laird Norton initiated an annual business meeting that included all family members. Specially designed programs for the children soon followed, to coincide with the sessions scheduled for their parents. Policies were written to further professionalize management, establish nomination criteria, expand communications, and open up opportunities for family members to serve as resources and contributors in the expanding family functions. On the business side, the company's dividends increased dramatically.

Laird Norton demonstrated its commitment to change by establishing term limits for the president's job, and when Nathalie stepped down in 1994, her cousin, Tim Taylor, took over, making his own mark as an innovative and inclusive leader.

Clearly the leaders of Laird Norton have believed that innovation could come from anywhere and have created an environment to encourage family members to offer their ideas for advancing the company. This spirit of change is tempered by a set of core values, one of which was expressed by Nathalie when she articulated the fifth generation's desire to serve as stewards of the company "for our children, and our children's children."

In the next chapter, we discuss in depth how the CEO— particularly the new successor to leadership—can create an environment that fosters and embraces change.

Chapter 5

Leading Change in a Family Firm

A Guide for the Successor

The foremost responsibility of a new leader in a family business is to preserve the best of the past while at the same time opening up the organization so that it is willing and able to accept and embrace continuous change. Mastering this paradoxical challenge is, we believe, central to the success of successor leadership.

When a new leader takes the helm of a company, the organization is likely to be at its highest level of anxiety. Employees and family members alike may feel a sense of loss of what has been a familiar leadership style for perhaps a whole generation and have many questions about what the company will be like (and what their lives will be like) under the new chief executive. Such anxiety makes the introduction of change and the creation of a culture of change even more difficult for the successor. In short, new leaders really have their work cut out for them—unless they are lucky enough to be successors in businesses that have already made change their tradition.

In our view, it is the job of the CEO not merely to run the business but to lead change. One family business we know offers this useful question: **"Are you working ON the company or are you working FOR the company?"** Working *for* the company means doing the day-to-day job of keeping things going. Working *on* the company means developing it in such a way that it is going to sustain itself into the future. The chief operating officer runs the company, thus working *for* the company. But there also needs to be somebody working *on* the company, envisioning its future and implementing the changes needed to get there. And that's the CEO.

A MODEL FOR LEADING CHANGE

The steps below can be viewed as a model for leading change. This model can give you some ways of thinking about change that may not have occurred to you before. Or it can be used as the tool with which you actually make change in your company. These are not steps to be done in chronological order. Rather, **they are processes that need to take place, often simultaneously, to promote successful change in a family business.** Please keep in mind that although we may speak of the "successor," we are also including multiple successors, such as sibling or cousin teams.

1. Understand the Fears and Needs of Others

As you have seen in Chapter 2, there are many impediments to change in a family firm. Often, these are rooted in the fears that people have. An outgoing or soon-to-be-outgoing CEO may worry that changes will threaten the success of the company and hurt him or her financially in retirement. Other family shareholders may also wonder how changes will affect the value of their shares in the company. Key non-family employees may be unhappy that the leader they've been serving for so long is leaving and may be reluctant to transfer their loyalty to a next-generation CEO who, they fear, will tamper with the outgoing leader's legacy.

A successor needs to understand and address the anxieties of those who seem to be obstructing or resisting change. That includes understanding whether an individual is truly obstructionistic or resistant, or is merely complacent because the business is enjoying success.

Here, in more detail, are some of the fears and needs experienced by people significant to a family business when new leadership takes over—and ways that a new leader can respond:

The Incumbent/Outgoing CEO. Incumbent chief executives—especially founding CEOs—may be concerned about their "place in history." Founders who view themselves as heroes may feel that "the company can't survive without me" and unconsciously hope the business dies after they're gone to prove what heroes they were.

Founders who have achieved financial comfort may not see the point of taking the risks that change requires. "I've got all the money I need," such an incumbent may reason. "If we are able to grow this business and increase its value, then I've just got more estate taxes to pay. Why the heck should I change?"

Or the incumbent may not feel financially comfortable and fears that making change is too risky and will threaten the security of his or her retirement years.

And, very commonly, incumbents may be experiencing a number of psychological stresses: they are older and are having to face their mortality; this business has been their life, and they don't know what they'll do with themselves if they retire; their status is changing—once they are no longer CEO, they won't be the center of attention and power, and they are probably not looking forward to that. Managing these issues requires a great deal of finesse on the part of the successor who wants to—indeed must—open the organization to change.

Dealing with the "heroic" founder and securing his or her blessing may require the successor to work on helping the founder see how he or she is going to be viewed by history—and to see how much more positive that view will be if the business continues to succeed in the future rather than fails after the founder is gone.

In essence, the successor must shape how the incumbent is going to be perceived. The successor can create ceremonies or begin to write documents—a family business history, perhaps—that say, "Here is what this person has left behind. Here is what this person has meant to the history of this company." In short, successors find ways to honor their predecessors and also help define new roles for the predecessors once they are no longer in charge—possibly a consulting or advisory role—to assure them that they continue to be valuable. The former chairman and CEO of ABARTA, a family-owned Pittsburgh-based conglomerate, John Bitzer Jr. says of his retirement: "Something that has helped make it work for me is that the third generation has treated me throughout the process with a respect and deference beyond what any person could or should expect. That has helped plenty."

To prevent parents' financial security—too much or too little—from becoming a roadblock to change, **next-generation leaders must help deal with the issue of helping the parents to become truly financially independent from the business, that thing they may have originally created in order to become**

financially independent. It means figuring out a way to be responsive to the parents' fears about long-term security. The successor may have to buy the business to give parents the financial security they need and earn the privilege to make changes.

Another way to help win the parents' blessing for change and their ability to let go is to demonstrate to them that the members of the next generation have a common vision and can work together. Many parents hang on out of fear that their children won't get along.

In sum, the best way to deal with incumbents' fear of change is to create the conditions under which change is not threatening to them. **If you assure that incumbents are financially secure and have made them comfortable about how history will view them, given them something to do that they find meaningful, and relieved them of the responsibility of managing next-generation conflicts, then you have made change as unthreatening as you possibly can.**

Other Family Members and Non-family Executives. As with a resistant incumbent CEO, the successor will want to identify the fears and needs of family members and key non-family executives who seem resistant to change. Is a sibling worried that Dad's legacy to the business will be disrespected and disregarded by the successor? Is a family shareholder fearful that the new leader, by making changes, will jeopardize a successful company's dividends? Is a non-family manager upset over the possibility that the next-generation leader doesn't understand and appreciate how much she contributed to the company in the early days, or so worried about her job security that she is encouraging the incumbent to stay in power?

In some cases, successors building their own management teams may need to find new roles for long-time non-family executives or even be forced to let recalcitrant ones go. But often, the key is addressing the fears of family members and talented non-family employees and, as Nathalie Simsak did at Laird Norton, engaging them in the process of change.

2. Demystify the Past

When you demystify the past, you clarify the past. You take what has been regarded as heroic on the part of Dad or Granddad and recast it in human terms. The successor's challenge is to put the spotlight on the fact that the predecessors had strong values and that one of those values was a willingness to change, a willingness to see the world differently, a willingness to swim upstream. But the successor must also get across the message that leaning on what the forebears did is dangerous. **You can demystify and depersonalize the reasons for past success by deflecting credit from the founder's unique brilliance to the organization's strengths and the founder's capacity to encourage innovation and change.** You can also keep communicating the message that while the predecessors may have been the heroes of the past, the current team members are the heroes of the present and future.

> You can demystify and depersonalize the reasons for past success by deflecting credit from the founder's unique brilliance to the organization's strengths and the founder's capacity to encourage innovation and change.

3. Build a Coalition for Change

Creating change is not something you can do alone. It requires others' support. When John M. Bissell "encouraged" certain family executives to leave BISSELL, Inc., he did so because he didn't want to block off all the top executive positions by filling them with family. He knew he couldn't attract or retain good outside executives unless they saw an opportunity for advancement. However, easing out family members represented a wrenching change for the company and probably could not have been accomplished were it not for the support of John's predecessor and the backing of the BISSELL board of directors.

Allies can come from many quarters: your siblings and cousins in the business; family members who are not employees but who may be stockholders; key non-family executives; the board of directors; outside advisors; suppliers; the outgoing CEO. Involve them in developing and articulating the vision for the future and enlist them collectively as advocates for the kind of change that is necessary to achieve that vision. You may need to demonstrate to some that the risk of not making change is greater than the risk of changing.

Sometimes, pruning will be required. **If people aren't willing or able to buy into a new vision and into the changes that are essential, providing mechanisms by which they can opt out— that is, buying out shareholders or offering early retirement to certain employees—is a very viable option.**

4. Create an Environment that Supports Change

An important part of creating an environment where change can thrive is building the foundation discussed in depth in Chapter 3. Stated simply, it means identifying and communicating the core values that are central to your corporate culture. Because core values rarely change, they offer family members and employees a sense of stability in a world that is undergoing constant and rapid change and provide them with a base from which they can initiate change themselves.

By putting the spotlight on their predecessors and honoring them instead of criticizing them, successors can set the stage for change. A successor, for example, can convey this message: "My predecessors did NOT say this was the only way to do things. Dad and Granddad were actually change agents, and they would want me to be the same. What each did when he ran the business was different from what was done before, and it was brilliant, given the time. But times change and what they would want for us now is to be able to adapt and be creative and be leaders for whatever time we're operating in." One of the values of the predecessors, the successor can point out, was a willingness to change.

CEOs also create an environment supporting change by honoring and celebrating people for challenging leadership with new ideas. Where in the past a company might have recognized employees for their loyalty and tireless effort, today it might instead recognize them for delegating and for empowering others. In much the same way, leaders can offer reinforcement to people for coming up with innovative ideas. Take, for example, Van Dyne-Crotty, Inc., a Dayton, Ohio–based industrial laundry company with 20 locations and 1,000 employees. Managers with the creativity to solve their own problems and the ability to forecast the financial impact of their suggestions are the ones who get moved up VDC's corporate ladder. The owning Crotty family also preaches the importance of making sure that all hires are more talented in some respect than their supervisors. That reinforces the idea that the primary role of managers is to facilitate good work, not to do it themselves.

5. Unfreeze, Introduce Change, Refreeze

There's a very powerful but simple model of change based on the work of many thinkers in the field of change. It stipulates that first, you unfreeze the organization, then you introduce new ideas, and finally you refreeze.

When you unfreeze the organization, the point is to create dissatisfaction with the current situation. This might be done by simply presenting disturbing information, without trying to offer a solution. Suppose you are the new leader of your family's toy company. The disturbing information you might present is the fact that sales were down 4 percent this quarter compared to a year ago, and game division sales were down 7 percent. Rather than judging the information and saying, "We've got to change our product mix," you start by simply putting the data out there to raise people's discomfort with the status quo.

New ideas can then be introduced in a number of ways. You can call on people such as consultants, advisors, or industry experts, who will bring in outside opinion that reinforces the need for change. You can then create a problem-solving task force made up of people within the company (but not including yourself) who can explore the issues, identify causes, and propose changes and solutions.

As the direction emerges, you can start to seek allies in the organization, opinion leaders to promote the changes that are needed. In other words, **change is subtly choreographed.** It is neither necessary nor desirable for you to stand up in front of employees and say, "We've got to change this, so we're going to do this and we're going to do that." The process is one of letting the members of the organization come to the realization that there are problems, and letting other leaders convince employees what steps must be taken and what changes made.

"Refreezing" means reinforcing desirable behaviors. For example, suppose it's been determined that the company needs to be more customer-service oriented. When a particular employee provides exemplary customer service, that gets recognized and celebrated. That helps others to see what will be rewarded in your company. Even if employees stumble when they are trying to provide good customer service, you still reinforce their effort. You basically say, "What you're trying to do is great. Don't worry about how it's working out yet."

Celebrate successes as soon as they occur. When good service results in a new sale or in more sales to an existing customer, let everyone know the good news. Some other ways to refreeze include revamping your compensation system and readjusting your performance review forms to reinforce the new behaviors.

Scenarios Help!

When you're going through a period of uncertainty, one of the exercises that will help you and your key managers or other employees imagine the future is to paint alternative pictures of the future. For example, you might come up with views of what would happen to the company if Internet sales grabbed a huge market share. A second scenario might be that consumers are working more in isolation so they are increasingly eager to get out and shop in a social environment. How might that affect your company?

Scenarios help an organization to unfreeze and to imagine alternative futures that may help it find the right answers to questions about which there is, right now, still too little information.

---

6. Seek Incremental Change

Unless the family is in immediate danger, evolutionary change is not the goal, and, in our view, a successor in a family business should not attempt to foment revolution. In the first place, a revolutionary approach may simply harden the resistance of those in the family and in the business who are the least likely to welcome change. And, in the second, revolutionary change is probably just too risky.

Successors can be more successful if they employ what we call "strategic incrementalism" instead of making fundamental change. Fundamental change means throwing out the old strategy completely and adopting a new one. Incremental change means testing elements in your strategy and adopting smaller changes as they prove successful. For example, suppose you own a grocery store. A fundamental change would be to sell the store and go into a grocery home-delivery business. An incremental change would be to test home delivery from your existing store and, if successful, add it to your service. Or, say your family has a construction business. With the thought of testing the market, your company takes a job in a county that it hasn't worked in before. You're not making a commitment; there are no plans to open an office there. You're just going outside your normal practice, testing something out, hoping to learn, learning to accept it if it doesn't work out, not risking a lot, and not raising a lot of expectations. That's strategic incrementalism.

Remember when the family-controlled *New York Times*, the once "Old Gray Lady," added color to its pages? Some feared that with color, the *Times* would no longer appear dignified and serious enough and that it would lose its credibility. But the *Times* added color to meet the competition, and it has continued to thrive. It did not, after all, turn itself into *USA Today*.

7. Reinforce What's *Not* Going to Change

The human need for the comfort of stability suggests that even when the goal is to make change your tradition, **it's important to**

make clear to employees and family members—and probably to customers, suppliers, and other stakeholders as well—**what's not going to change.** For example, what was not going to change at the *New York Times*, as fourth-generation Chairman and Publisher Arthur Ochs Sulzberger Jr. made clear, was their standard of journalistic excellence.

As we've made clear in Chapter 3, the foundation of values on which a family business is built is rarely going to change. And in the midst of change that is swirling around in a family business, a new leader needs to communicate reassurances about what will remain stable.

But be truthful. If you can truthfully say, "These changes are not going to affect anybody's compensation for the next two years," say it. If you can't truthfully say, "Don't worry, nobody's job is at risk," don't say it. Instead, you might want to say something like, "One thing that won't change is our open-door policy for anyone who has a concern or worry."

WHAT THE SUCCESSOR NEEDS TO PULL IT OFF

Successors who effectively lead change in family firms have accomplished much. The job is that tough, and the characteristics that such leaders are naturally blessed with or take time and energy to develop mean that they are extremely mature individuals. The phrase "emotionally intelligent" could have been coined just for them.

One thing successors must do is make the business—not themselves—important. They need to be able to accept and be comfortable with and enthusiastic about seeing themselves

EXHIBIT 5   A Leader's Model for Creating Change

1. Understand and address the fears and needs of those who are resistant to change.
2. Demystify the past by focusing not on the predecessors' heroics but on their willingness to innovate.
3. Don't go it alone. Build a coalition of supporters.
4. Create an environment that supports change—one that is built on a foundation of core values and recognizes people for new ideas.
5. "Unfreeze" the organization by presenting disturbing facts that call for action; encourage and introduce new ideas; "refreeze" by reinforcing desired new behavior and celebrating successes.
6. Engage in "strategic incrementalism," making small changes and testing their viability.
7. Reassure people about what will not change.

as leaders of culture more than as leaders of decision making, strategies, and action. This calls for understated, behind-the-scenes leadership. And that usually doesn't win attention or praise. It's not very dramatic, and no one says, "Wow, look what you did!"

But in truth, changes wrought by such leaders may be dramatic indeed. Consider, for instance, the achievements of Jimmy Cleveland Jr., third-generation president and CEO of Atlanta-based Cleveland Group.

Cleveland Group's origins lie in Cleveland Electric, founded in 1925 by Jimmy's grandfather, Ras. The little company repaired electric motors—a solid niche with room to grow, given Atlanta's hot, muggy weather and the numerous cotton mills in outlying areas. With offices, plants, and warehouses requiring fans to cool the air and electric motors to power machinery, many motors needed repair, and business was plentiful. The company's reputation for quality and reliability grew, as did its ability to work with larger motors. It broadened its territory, sending trucks on daily routes collecting motors and other electrical apparatus for repair, and responding to critical, on-site electrical repair needs. Maintenance people in the Cleveland-serviced facilities began requesting parts, thus expanding Cleveland into the electrical parts distribution business.

By 1990, under the leadership of Ras's sons, Louis and James, the family's Cleveland Electric Company included motor repair, distribution, sales and service, and mechanical and electrical contracting housed in facilities in several states. The Cleveland Group holding company umbrella included the "motor repair shop," nurtured by Jimmy's Uncle Louis, a substantial electrical and mechanical contracting company developed by Jimmy's father, Jimmy Sr., and Aviation Constructors, Inc., a general contracting and construction management company in the aviation industry organized in 1987. Three generations of Cleveland's were actively involved. The family's values—service to employees, customers, communities, and shareholders; stewardship of financial, physical, and human assets; excellence in product production, service conduct, management, and all other aspects of the company; maintenance of high character standards; and a high level of competence in leadership—permeated the organization from top to bottom. Many employees had spent their entire working lives with Cleveland.

In a decade of massive changes beginning in 1990, the company redeemed the shares of 16 out of 25 family owners, restructured the company, implemented an active board with outside directors, accomplished a generational transition, introduced total quality management and achieved ISO certification, got up to speed on strategic planning and other forward-looking methodologies, totally revamped the company's information system, moved four fourth-generation family members into leadership positions, and much more.

But despite the apparent external strength of the business, Jimmy Cleveland knew more was necessary. Before him lay the change that was perhaps most difficult—the sale of the original business, nurtured by his grandfather and then his uncle for more than 70 years. The motor repair business required expensive capital equipment to operate in an industry rapidly changing due to innovations in electronics and disposable motors. Slow growth and poor returns attracted little interest from the fourth generation, while meeting the challenges of change increasingly demanded scarce resources of funds and stretched executive attention.

Still, Jimmy moved very slowly. He carefully built consensus among owners and directors. When it came, the vote to put the "motor shop" on the block was unanimous, as was the acceptance of the ultimate buyer's offer.

To reach that point, Jimmy had quietly and patiently worked to refocus the family's thinking, acting with great sensitivity to the emotional issues involved and respect for past accomplishments. He took advantage of the insights and advice of outside directors, encouraging them to share their views with all shareholders. He invited the younger generation to all board meetings and solicited their input. Over time, he successfully built consensus among all generations and family branches.

Three or four years elapsed from the first thought of selling to the final decision to sell. Explained Jimmy: "Another businessman might have made the decision three years earlier and forced the issue, but out of deference to my uncle and in the interest of family harmony, I wanted everyone to have time to become comfortable with the need to sell. The input of our outside directors, who had been expressing their views about selling for some time, helped bring all family members around, as did the opinions of the fourth generation."

In 1998, the motor repair and new equipment divisions were sold, allowing the company to focus exclusively on its contracting and service businesses. The effect of the sale? "The financial picture immediately improved, the funds allowed us to pay down debt, it freed my time to concentrate on the business I knew best, and allowed us to take advantage of other opportunities and to develop a profitable strategic focus," Jimmy said. Both 1999 and 2000 were outstanding in terms of sales and profits.

With his major change goals accomplished, Jimmy turned to preparing for his own retirement and succession to the fourth generation represented by two sons, a nephew, and a cousin's son. "We have a wonderfully talented, diverse group. They're all smart and all highly motivated . . . The organizational structure is not yet finalized," says Jimmy, once again exhibiting patience. "We're letting the cream rise to the top." Their job will be easier because, at Cleveland Group, change has now become the tradition.

While the old adage, "slow and steady wins the race," might seem to apply only to Jimmy's success, his willingness to proceed in a "slow and steady" manner also indicates the depth of his conviction that he was doing the right thing for the company and his concern for maintaining harmonious relationships within his family.

Like Jimmy Cleveland, successors must know themselves extremely well and have great internal strength if they are to be able to distinguish change driven by the family business's agenda versus change responsive to their personal agendas. To gain this kind of self-knowledge generally requires having independent, significant success outside the company. It also means getting honest feedback from a support group of peers—preferably from sources outside the business or family, such as a board of directors, consultants, industry share groups, or advisors. These outside sources can also help successors address their own anxieties as they are leading change. You can't really trust yourself or those inside the organization for honest feedback during such a period of uneasiness. This is where independent directors can be especially precious.

We find that successful change leaders have great self-confidence as well as security in their own identity. They really believe that the continuity of the enterprise is important and that credit for themselves is unimportant. In the minds of other family members, they are very trustworthy. In addition, they are excellent communicators, able to convey ideas and abstract messages in "sound bites" or short speeches. They are consistent. And they have a supportive temperament—they are able to comfort people through the discomfort of change.

Change leaders are comfortable with the idea that they do not always have to be perceived as "doers." They understand that they are still doing their job if they take a long walk just to think about things. This requires special strength on the part of sons and daughters of entrepreneurial parents, who may feel that successors are not earning their keep unless they are acting and doing all the time.

The best change leaders we know understand how culture affects people. They understand human behavior and are able to see human beings as part of a system. They also understand history and symbolism. We recall one leader who was trying to get across the message that the company really needed to break down its "silos"—that is, people confined to their own departments—and increase interaction. When the Berlin Wall came down, she bought a large chunk of it, broke it up into little pieces, gave everybody a small piece at a company meeting, and said, "We've got to break the walls down around here." At a company retreat, another family business leader passed around T-shirts with a picture of the world on them in order to get across the message, "We have to start thinking globally."

Successful successors in family businesses know that they don't have to be the source of all the new ideas. In fact, they understand that the less they are seen as the source of ideas, the better. They know that the collective wisdom of the organization is greater than the wisdom of any one person, and when more people participate, there is more buy-in to more new ideas. **It's the successor's job not to create all the ideas in the company but to create the environment that encourages them.**

As you can see, successors face an extremely complex and difficult challenge when it comes to creating a tradition of change. No matter how right or smart they may be, they lack credibility because they are younger and less experienced. At the same time, they may face resistance from siblings, non-family executives, advisors, and—most intimidating of all—their parents. To be a champion of change under such circumstances may appear to be a fool's errand. But don't be discouraged. We've seen successors meeting this challenge successfully many, many times.

EXHIBIT 6   Desirable Characteristics of Change Leaders

Change Leaders ...

- Know themselves very well and embody self-confidence, inner strength, and integrity;
- Make the business more important than themselves;
- Enthusiastically embrace being behind-the-scenes, understated leaders of culture rather than visible decision makers;
- Recognize the need for change but respect the past;
- Continuously adapt the company to what it needs to be in the future;
- Exemplify genuine concern with the long-term viability and long-term perspective of the company;
- Have broad education and experience that includes significant success outside the family business;
- Are consensus builders;
- Serve as educators to family members and employees;
- Turn to trusted independent board members, advisors, or family members for honest feedback.

Chapter 6

Managing Resources for Change

How you manage your resources—people, money, facilities, equipment, and so on—has a great deal of influence on your ability to change and to do it in a timely, appropriate, and profitable fashion.

Good, solid family businesses, even relatively small ones, can be very successful and can generate substantial resources. Consider the generation of cash, for example. If profits are used in certain ways—to enrich owners and allow them to live a high lifestyle, to provide jobs to family members who aren't very productive, or to implement a no-debt policy or maintain a cash hoard in the business—then money may not be available to fund necessary change. Not only are significant opportunities drained away by the poor use of cash, but the poor use of cash may support dubious human resource practices.

Owners who hoard cash in their businesses may be doing so to insulate and protect their companies. But in many such cases, the business becomes overcapitalized. Better, in our view, to use some of that cushion to provide independent financial security to the older generation, which allows them to let go of control so that change can be introduced. Funds can also be used to fund strategic experiments that generate incremental change.

The really smart family business owners we know are typically somewhat modest in their lifestyles and are not focused on consumption. They are also disciplined in terms of using the business for family goals, being careful to employ only those family members who can make a contribution to the business. And they are very conscious of the need to use their war chest to finance change. **Their budgets include plans for strategic reinvestment and strategic experimentation in the business.**

For example, the Lanier family, owners of Interstate Telephone Company, used the excess cash flow of their small telephone company in West Point, Georgia, to respond to threatening deregulation by getting into niche telecommunication markets. Before taking the riskier path of change, family owners who were nervous about the change could sell their shares. Many did. ITC Holding Company became one of the first resellers of long-distance telephone service and came up with the first voice-mailbox answering service owned by an independent telephone company. Both of these businesses were later sold to larger telecommunications companies. In so doing, the family learned to recognize promising innovations in their industry. The family's wise use of cash has enabled it to change with the times and to become one of the leading venture capitalists in the telecommunications field. Recent investments in Mindspring, an Internet service provider, and Powertel, a cellular communications company, netted the family over $1 billion when those companies merged with larger competitors. In other words, in a period of about 20 years, the family became a major player in a world full of AT&Ts, MCIs, merging Baby Bells, and giant cable companies, all because it decided to concentrate some of its excess cash flow on becoming more entrepreneurial and taking advantage of opportunities to change. Throughout the change, however, family leaders remained true to strong core values passed from generation to generation (see the Smith Lanier interview in the *Family Business Advisor's* June 1998 issue).

NEEDED: A NEW ATTITUDE TOWARD FINANCE

When it comes to finance, no family business has the luxury of hoarding cash forever. Time will force the issue. We find that when a family firm reaches the third or fourth generation, it typically runs out of cash, and the owners must rethink how to finance the business. Change is thrust upon them.

As the business and the family each get older and bigger, certain things become inevitable: even with the best of estate planning, the family will have to face death taxes; the business

---

EXHIBIT 7   Building Blocks of Change in a Family Firm

+ An incumbent generation promoting change
+ A younger generation that gains education and experience outside the family business and brings back new ideas
+ Family members inside and outside the business who are educated to understand the need for change and the process of change
+ A coalition of family members, key non-family executives, and independent board members who endorse change
+ An organizational spirit or culture that supports innovation and experimentation
+ A family commitment to managing business resources in a way that maximizes change while minimizing risk
+ Recognition that the business of origin may one day have to be replaced by more relevant strategies and ventures

must change and transform; capital will be needed to grow or start new businesses; and very likely, by this time, one or more family members will want to be bought out. All of these monetary matters place great demands on the business for capital, demands that usually exceed a private family business's financial resources.

Because they want to maintain as much independence as possible, many family businesses we know tend to reject some of the obvious possibilities for raising cash—going public, seeking outside private investors, or taking on an equity or joint venture partner. They also resist the notion of going to the bank and borrowing more money than they're used to borrowing. Another possibility is to sell part of the business, and while doing so is not unusual, some families just don't like that option.

The point is, **many families have to change their attitudes about financing their businesses—their financing paradigms—to find sources of capital that they haven't so far needed to find.** In doing so, family members may need to stretch beyond their comfort zones as well as their culture. A **"no-debt" tradition, for example, just may not work anymore.**

One option is to develop a different strategic perspective about your business. Perhaps over time, you change your business so that it becomes less capital intensive. For example, if your business requires enormous sums of capital to build new facilities or purchase new equipment, you might change the business from being one that builds and owns facilities to one that operates facilities that other people own. The Marriott Corporation has done just that. A good operator of hotels, it learned that it didn't need to own all the hotels it operated. Instead, the company put its highly regarded family name on hotels owned by others and began to make profits from being the operators.

Many families have to change their attitudes about financing their businesses—their financing paradigms—to find sources of capital that they haven't so far needed to find.

Another family business we know that traditionally used its own capital to finance real estate developments for the family's own portfolio, began to invite others to invest in specific projects. Construction and property management fees charged to the projects became significant new sources of income.

You may find business growth strategies that require a smaller percentage of capital than you needed in the past—leasing property or equipment instead of buying it, for example, or shifting your business to being less of a manufacturing business and more of a service business. Rather than building a new factory, for instance, we know a family business that contracted for the production of an existing Latin American facility.

Families that are very clever, farsighted, and successful are aware of the fact that eventually, they are going to need more capital than they have traditionally had access to. We find that they are often very creative in adapting the business or adapting their attitudes toward the business in ways that allow them to get access to new money using different means than they have thought about in the past. Some find ways to use other people's money without compromising their goals or their interests, and others change themselves culturally to become more comfortable using debt or using partners or selling a part of their business once in a while. They realize that these methods can be the way to keep the business in the family and to keep it thriving. (For more information about finance and family business, please see the Family Business Leadership

Series title *Financing Transitions: Managing Capital and Liquidity in the Family Business.*)

You don't want to wait until the third or fourth generation, however, before you acquire the greater financial sophistication that these rapidly changing times demand. A number of financial issues require a family's attention no matter what stage of business it is in, including looking at your dividend policies and practices and how they affect your company's ability to be innovative, what financial strategy you should follow in order to change and grow, and where you can secure financial resources for the future. If your company does not already have a thoroughly trained and experienced chief financial officer, it's time to consider hiring one. **Helping family shareholders who are not in the business to understand such concepts as "return on investment" and "debt-to-equity ratios" is also very important.** As one third-generation CEO told us: "I used to think that arguing over valuation methodologies with my cousins would be my worst nightmare. But it turned out to be a rather stimulating and enlightening discussion."

STRUCTURING YOUR COMPANY FOR CHANGE

Another element of managing human resources for change is to consider how your organization is structured. **Many relatively small family businesses are hesitant to develop middle management, for example, because they see managers as expensive "overhead." The owners of such businesses try to do everything themselves. Besides the fact that they can't do everything themselves, they don't have the time to think strategically and generate new ideas. They build a trap that makes it impossible for the company to change.**

As we indicated earlier, we take the view that **the job of the chief executive officer is not merely to run the company but**

to lead change. If you are the CEO, it makes sense to invest in enough executive talent to allow you or some other appropriate person time to envision the future and work toward implementing that future as opposed to being totally eaten up by day-to-day operating concerns.

Begin by understanding that the different titles or different roles in companies are REAL. Being chairman is a real job, and that job is to manage the board of directors, lead the shareholders, and guide the business's values. Being the chief operating officer (or, in some companies, the executive vice president) is a real job, and that job is to run current operations.

The CEO has a real job, too. You oversee the COO, but more importantly, you plan for and implement the future. As the executive responsible for building the business's value, the CEO should spend more time working *on* the business than working *for* the business. And that means being responsible for continuous improvement—in short, for change.

As your company grows, you need a more fully articulated upper- and middle-management team. Where you may have had an accounting manager that you called your chief financial officer, for example, you now hire a real CFO who can be part of your strategic team in planning the future and who can manage the more sophisticated approach to finance that's required to take the company forward.

The job of the chief executive officer is not merely to run the company but to lead change.

You'll be investing more money, but you won't be buying mere "overhead." You'll be bringing more highly talented people into your organization and giving them more power and more responsibility and counting on them for being part of the process that recognizes, plans, and implements changes that build value.

The Crotty family of Van Dyne-Crotty, Inc., which was discussed in Chapter 5, has focused heavily on professionalizing its business, hiring and developing the best managers it can. That enables family members to be more philosophical. "We're more geared toward issues of vision, strategy, and direction," explained Dan Crotty, the third-generation CEO.

You can't have the ability to address or create change effectively without the wise allocation of resources. That means a commitment to thinking and rethinking the way you deploy resources and adapting your views to meet the needs of change.

Chapter 7

A Word to the Outgoing CEO

If you are the incumbent CEO, one whose retirement may be in sight and who is diligently bringing along your successor(s), you will want to do everything in your power to turn over a healthy organization. One of the marks of a healthy organization is the ability to change. And you, as the senior-generation CEO, have a great deal of influence on whether or not your family business has that ability.

As we have said earlier in this book, it's a fortunate successor who takes over leadership of a company that has already made change its tradition. Even if it has not, you still can do much to ready the organization for change and to support your successors in the changes they must make when they rise to leadership.

First, if you have not already done so, we encourage you to read Chapter 5, "Leading Change in a Family Firm: A Guide for the Successor," which is addressed to the next-generation leader. From it, you will see how we think change should be approached. Perhaps you will draw comfort from the fact that we think change should be incremental, not revolutionary or unnecessarily risky. You will also gain an understanding of the job of your successor, which will be considerably unlike your job, especially if you were the founder of the business.

One of the greatest gifts you can give to your successors and to your business in the time you have left as CEO is to take some steps that will help prevent crises as the transition from your generation to the next generation takes place.

The first step is to arm yourself with knowledge about change. You are beginning to do that by reading this book. If you are in your 60s or 70s or even in your late 50s, you come from an era that represents the winding down of the Industrial Age. As we discussed in Chapter 1, this was a time of greater stability. Things changed but not nearly so fast as they do now. People in their 30s, perhaps your sons and daughters, represent the Information Age and the New Economy. The world has changed so much that it is simply not realistic to expect that they can or ought to run a business the way their parents have run it. By understanding this, you go a long way toward preventing conflicts over how the business should be run and the changes the next generation will bring. If you are the business's founder, it's very likely that you lead in a strong, entrepreneurial style, one that is forceful, assertive, and decisive. A member of the next generation, however, more likely will seek to create consensus around change and concentrate on building teamwork. He or she may be understated. That may not look like leadership to you, but it is. And it's a style of leadership that works very well for successors in a family firm.

A second step, and a particularly challenging one if you are the founder, is to avoid presenting yourself as the "hero" of the organization. Founders are almost always regarded as heroes—you are probably no exception. And it's gratifying to be regarded that way. But others in the family, particularly key non-family executives and family members who are not in the business, may have doubts and fears about the company's ability to continue

EXHIBIT 8   Ideal Incumbents

* See themselves as responsible for creating and maintaining a climate of change
* Challenge, encourage, and empower the next generation to introduce change (while maintaining their judgment and power to veto inappropriate change—using counsel of the board)
* Use their experience to guide change rather than resist it
* Believe the company can survive without them and discourage being perceived as "heroes"
* Recognize that a successor's job is to build consensus around change and to forge a team

successfully once the hero retires. **You can do much to calm these fears and pave the way for the future by downplaying any heroic role attributable to you and giving your successors increased responsibility, visibility, and recognition.**

Most important, however, is to encourage, challenge, and empower your successors to bring about change. We held our breath at one family business retreat, when cousin-members of the successor generation presented their vision for the future. We knew one of the fathers could be extremely critical, but we exhaled with relief when the presentation was done, and he stood up with a smile and said, "It's a new day."

Another way to support your successor is to prepare your key non-family executives for change. Some of them have no doubt been with you for many, many years and are deeply loyal to you. The transition to a new generation of leadership may be eased for them if, well ahead of your retirement, you support, in their presence, the new ideas that the next generation is bringing into the company. Gently but firmly and continuously make it clear to non-family managers that you embrace change and that it is part of their job to do the same.

> "Another kind of hero revitalizes the tradition by re-interpreting it to make its meaning valid and alive . . . "
>
> —Joseph Campbell

Similarly, as the incumbent CEO, you can help prepare family members for change by discussing the need for change and giving it and your successors your blessing at family council meetings and in everyday conversation.

One delicate subject that we have touched on earlier is the tenure of the CEO and how, if it's too long, it can be a hindrance to change. Only you can decide whether to retire sooner rather than later. **Many CEOs in their 60s and 70s will say, "Gee, I still have something left in me." That is not necessarily the standard for staying on as CEO. Using the familiar analogy of the relay race, our experience suggests that the baton is best passed when both runners are going at full speed, not when the first has stumbled and fallen and has nothing left to give.**

"I've challenged myself to build a life largely apart from the business," John Bitzer Jr., the former ABARTA CEO, once said about his own process of letting go. "It's my observation that this is the toughest part for a lot of people in this situation—to sustain a sense of personal worth without the trappings of the job and the business. This is why many stay around too long . . . and it's not a good reason to do so."

One more thing. Nearly every family firm we know eventually has to dramatically redefine the business it's in. It will suffer and perhaps fail completely if it sticks to the notion that "Granddad founded a widget company, and we're still going to make widgets," when the world's need for widgets has diminished.

If you are the founder, it helps enormously if you convey the message that the family firm is not in the business of making the product or delivering the service that you started out with. Instead, we encourage you to adopt and convey a mentality that says, "We are a family that pursues new ideas," instead of "We are the widget family." By doing so, you relieve your heirs of any guilt they might feel in not pursuing your dream and give them the permission and the freedom and the opportunity to make decisions that will enhance the health of the company.

In short, you can best foster change in your family business by thinking of yourself as a change agent. Take responsibility for change yourself by encouraging the next generation, perhaps as a task force of siblings or cousins, to develop a vision for the business based on their view of the future. Be open to their ideas and, as appropriate, encourage them to implement change. Remember how much power you have, even informally, as a parent, and use that power wisely and well. Be a supporter, not an impediment.

As one CEO told his 30-something children, niece, and cousin, "I'll be glad to hand over the business as soon as you can tell the board to its satisfaction what you hope to do with the business and how you plan to go about it." They did, and he did.

Chapter 8

Creating a Tradition of Change

To create a tradition of change in a family business, you must develop a **culture of change.** In other words, you need to put together an environment that embraces change, encourages it, and thrives on it. In a culture of change, an organization is flexible and adaptable. You can have continuous incremental and relatively painless change rather than facing the need to make wrenching change in order to survive. Change becomes a given, a constant. It's expected.

In Chapter 5, we outlined a model for change. Adopting and using that model again and again will support your effort to create an ongoing culture of change. But there are other actions family members can take to create and sustain a culture of change—individually as family members and non-family managers, and collectively as a family. Here are some ideas for making change your tradition:

♦ **Begin with yourself.** Because family businesses are tightly linked systems, an individual who changes what he or she does with persistence, consistency, and patience will find that others will change as well. For example, if you are a successor and you become less dependent on parents for approval, your parents and siblings are eventually likely to react accordingly. Your parents may find it easier to let go of control, and your siblings may begin to respect you as a more independent, mature person.

If you are a non-family executive, you might try re-examining any tendency to be skeptical about the successor or resistant to the changes he or she is trying to initiate. You are an opinion leader in the company, and the successor needs you to support change. When you give that support and participate in change, you reinforce the culture of change. (Not only that, but your life in the company under a new leader will probably become easier!)

If you are a sibling or a spouse who is not active in the business, find out what you can do to support change in the company. Can you speak positively of change in conversations with other family members? Can you organize discussions about change and its importance at family council meetings? Can you educate yourself about the business so that you better understand why change is necessary?

EXHIBIT 9   Five Ways to Keep Your Strategy Fresh

1. Include three or four active CEOs of vibrant firms on your board.
2. Make way for new people, regularly, at all levels of the organization.
3. Earmark funds each year for developing new products or services, new markets, or new ways of doing business.
4. Host a "strategic think tank" once a year; bring in experts to brainstorm about trends and new ideas.
5. Allow as many people as possible to have independent profit centers.

Do you harbor any feelings of sibling rivalry that might be getting in the way of supporting a successor who is trying to lead change? Can you put those feelings in check and give your support? What a difference that might make.

Changing oneself takes time and can be difficult. But the rewards of a successful family business are worth the effort. You may also find that relationships with colleagues and family members improve.

◆ **Challenge assumptions about CEO tenure.** Several times in this book we have touched on the fact that the lengthy tenures of CEOs in family businesses can result in stagnation in a company. Has that happened in your company? As we mentioned in Chapter 2, Roy Richards Jr., the second-generation CEO of Southwire Corp., urges family businesses to change leadership every ten years. In some companies where the next generation is not yet ready to take the reins, a CEO may pass on leadership to a younger sibling or cousin. While this is not always possible, it's something to think about.

◆ **Keep your strategy and culture fresh.** This is not only necessary, but it also sends a message throughout the organization that the family business is committed to embracing and meeting the challenge of change. Here are ways to keep your strategy fresh and your culture responsive:

1. Include three or four active CEOs of vibrant firms on your board.
2. Find ways to provide room for new people, regularly, at all levels of the organization. Studies suggest that companies benefit from having 25 percent to 35 percent new faces, every five years, at each level of the management structure— from entry-level managers to the executive committee.

3. Set "new business" goals, such as 15 percent of revenues from products younger than three years, or 10 percent of gross profits each year from new customers, and so on.

4. Determine a strategic budget of funds to be invested each year in new services, new markets, or new ways of doing business. Get into the habit of earmarking funds to test incremental change.

5. Emphasize *change* as fundamental to your culture. Frequently remind the organization about successful past changes and the need for continuing change.

6. Host a "strategic think tank" once a year with industry or business experts brainstorming about trends and new ideas.

7. Require that all family members in the business and key non-family executives spend significant time in the marketplace—with existing customers as well as potential customers.

8. Organize to allow as many people as possible to have independent profit centers.

9. Insist on business development plans for each profit center and meet with profit center managers individually once a month to discuss their strategic assumptions and progress.

◆ **Set an example.** Family business leaders reinforce a culture of change when they demonstrate a penchant for innovation. Reflecting on the role of a chairman in a family business, Robert J. R. Follett says that to him, fostering innovation was once merely an interesting pursuit. "Now, envisioning the future is a critical survival skill," says Follett, chairman emeritus of Follett Corporation, a fourth-generation family business best known for its more than 500 college bookstores.

Today, he says, a chairman "must set an example by being openly willing to consider the replacement of the company's current businesses with entirely new ventures."

◆ **Legitimize constant change.** How can a family business instill in employees the willingness to endure the discomfort of change and encourage them to work every day to find ways to do things better? Appeals to loyalty and security have limited impact. We find that those business owners who bring real meaning and positive energy to change and constant improvement personally believe that they are actually helping their employees be better people, adding to their self-esteem or training them for a more productive personal future.

Others see their business as having an important social purpose. Therefore, employees learn to believe that what they are doing is not important just for competitive success but for some good to the community or society.

In a family business, the strongest motivations come from "a cause" that employees believe in. When that "cause" is also a genuine passion shared by the business's owners and leaders, the business tends to be characterized by high employee energy, higher profitability, greater adaptability, and greater long-term employment security.

◆ **Communicate to reinforce your culture of change.** Use every means you have—newsletters and other publications, memos, electronic media, management and companywide meetings, planning retreats, family council meetings, dinner conversations, your own personal actions—to continually instill the benefits of change. Your in-house publication can feature the work of innovative employees, for example, or your website can tell the world about your newest products and services or ways of doing business. Be sure you communicate with family owners as well as employees.

We've known family business leaders to come up with ingenious ideas facilitating change. You can, too. One entrepreneur in his 60s, for example, has consciously hired key non-family executives who are around his son's age. In doing so, he has built a cadre of younger people who will be ready to become the team that leads change when the son takes over. The father struggles with change himself, but he has had the courage to recognize that change is needed.

Keep reminding yourself that a major theme of your family business's culture is change, and keep reinforcing that theme at every opportunity.

EXHIBIT 10   Change Is Easier When You . . .

- Assure that the senior generation has financial security that doesn't depend on the business.
- Talk about values as a family and know what you stand for.
- Reinterpret values to make them relevant to today's needs.
- Invite and listen to new ideas from employees at all levels.
- Get input from family members, your board, and your advisors.
- Focus the company on being a learning organization, bringing knowledge in from the outside world.

Chapter 9

Summary

The trick in a family business is to balance tradition with creativity and change with stability. Today's family businesses must manage the challenge of renewing their strategies at a much more frequent pace while at the same time preserving and reinterpreting for today the values that are dear to the family and that are the heart of the business. These tasks are essential to passing on a healthy business to the next generation.

It is the responsibility of each new generation to bring strategic renewal to a family business. The leader of the past could afford the luxury of bringing just one major strategy to a business during his or her generation-long tenure because change took place much more slowly. Today's family business leaders must find ways to renew their companies again and again. This means creating and sustaining a culture in which change is the norm and everybody, not just the CEO, is encouraged to take responsibility for new ideas and their implementation. It also means taking continuous steps to ensure that the company is a "learning" organization, in which everyone individually and collectively is encouraged on an ongoing basis to reach out for new ideas and information and bring what they've learned back to the company.

To embrace change most effectively, family business leaders may find that they and their companies need to be more open than they have been in the past. Family business owners have had a reputation for being secretive, but that may be changing as businesses adapt to meet current needs. Without being critical of their parents, the members of a next-generation cousin and sibling team announced their intentions of being more open and of being held more accountable than their fathers were. Because the young people had gone out of their way at the same time to praise and show respect for their fathers' accomplishments in the business, the fathers were not offended and warmly accepted their sons' plans.

We encourage successor leaders to make the institutionalization of change their primary focus. At the same time, we urge them to celebrate and honor the past without being bound by it and to find ways, when appropriate, to adapt traditions to contemporary realities.

We encourage outgoing CEOs to challenge and empower the next generation to create change and to support and welcome younger people's ideas. Outgoing CEOs exert considerable power for the good of a family firm when they acknowledge the fact that the company may not be able to stay in its original business forever and instill instead an attitude of "We're in the business of business." That gives future generations room to change business strategies without feeling disloyal to their predecessors.

Ultimately, making change the tradition of a family business is everybody's job.

We encourage non-family executives and family members not active in the business to be open to and to support change that successor leaders must bring. We recognize that this is not easy, but it is essential. Bringing about necessary change is the most important job a successor can do, and your understanding and appreciation of that fact will go a long way to benefit the business.

Ultimately, making change the tradition of a family business is everybody's job. And while change can be difficult, unsettling, and stressful, it can also be exhilarating. It prepares us for the future and makes us feel alive.

.

Index

ABARTA, 42, 70
Accounting manager, 65
Adaptability, 3, 77
Advice, 53
Advisors, 45, 47, 55, 56, 57, 78
Alar pesticide, 34
Allies, 45, 47
Al. Neyer, Inc., 24, 26–27
  Core Values, 26
*American Heritage Dictionary,
  The*, 21
AT&T, 60
Atlanta, GA, 51

Barilla, 35
Behavior, 23, 30–31
Bissell, Anna, 1
BISSELL, Inc., 1, 2–3, 34, 45
Bissell, John M., 2, 3, 4, 44
Bissell, Melville, 1, 2, 3, 4
Bissell family, 1
Bitzer, John Jr., 42, 70
Board of directors, 4, 24, 36, 45,
  53–54, 55, 65
Brazil, 29
Brown, Kent, 28
Bureaucracy, 15
Business, view of, 5
Business culture, 13
Business families, 20

Business financial requirements,
  changes in, 62
Business leader tenures, 6, 10
Business meeting, annual, 37
Business methods, 63
Business of origin, 53, 61
Business owners, 35
Business practices, 12, 13, 14
Business size, change in, 61
Business values, 19. *See also* Values
Buyouts, 31
Buy–sell agreements, 35

Campbell, Joseph, 70
Capital to grow the business, 59, 60,
  62–64
Caplan, Freida, 16
Caplan, Karen, 16
Carpet sweeper, 1, 34
Carrollton, GA, 11
Cash, managing, 59–61
"Century of Success," 1
CEOs, 10, 11, 13, 14, 15, 16, 25,
  28, 33, 34, 36, 40–41, 43, 46,
  64–65, 70–71, 79
  accountability of, 11
  feelings of incumbent, 41
  ideal incumbent, 69
  outgoing, 4, 14, 45, 67–71, 80
  tenure effect, 10, 69, 75

Ceremonies, 42
CFO, 65
Change
  adapting to, 1
  agents, 46, 71
  balancing with stability, 79
  building blocks of, 61
  choreographing, 47
  creating, 1, 4, 14, 36, 44
  fostering, 71
  foundation for, 19
  impediments to, 10–17
  incremental, 48–49, 60, 76
  issues, 7
  leaders, characteristics of, 55, 57
  legitimizing, 77
  models, 40–51
  promoting, 61
  resistance to, 14, 19, 41, 43, 74
  source of, 33
  spirit of, 37
Children, 27, 37, 43
Cincinnati, OH, 24, 27
Cleveland, Jimmy Jr., 51–54
Cleveland, Jimmy Sr., 51
Cleveland, Louis, 52
Cleveland, Ras, 51
Cleveland Group, 51–54
Climate of change, 69
Coalition for change, 61
  building, 44–45 51
Columbus, OH, 27
Commitment to change, 37
Communication, 37, 60, 77
Communicators, 55
Community, 29
Company culture, 23
Company performance,
  declining, 35
Company perspective, long-term, 57
Company restructuring, 52
Compensation, 48
Complacency, 13

Conflicts, 35
Consensus, 25, 53, 57, 68
Constancy, 20
Consultants, 47, 55
Contemporary challenges, 30–31
Continuity, 20
Continuous renewal, 1
COO, 65
Core values, 22, 24, 25, 26, 28, 37,
  45, 61
Cousins, 36, 37, 75
  members of successor generation,
  69
  teams, 40
Creativity, 46
Crises, 34
Crotty, Dan, 66
Crotty family, 46, 66
Culture of change, 10, 15, 29, 39, 73,
  74, 76, 77
Custom, 21
Customers, 31, 36

Dad, 43, 46
Daughters, 55, 68
Dayton, OH, 46
Death, 33
Death taxes, 61
Debt
  taking on, 15, 30, 31
  using, 63
Debt-to-equity ratio, 64
Decision makers, 57
Decision making, 29, 51
de Geus, Arie, 21
Demystifying the past, 44, 51
Depersonalization, 44
Depression, the, 25
Disaster plans, 35
Disloyalty, 15
Disrespect, 14
Diversification, 34
Dividend policies, 64

Dividends, 35, 37, 43, 64
Doers, 55

Economy, changes in, 33–34
Education, 57, 61
  about the business, 74
Electronic marketplace, 5
Emotional intelligence, 50
Employees, 12, 14, 25, 30, 36, 39, 45, 47–48, 50, 52, 57, 77–78
  recognizing, 46
  taking care of, 30, 31
Employers, early retirement for, 45
Entrepreneurs, 35, 68, 78
Entry standards for family members, 2
Environment that supports change, creating, 36, 45–46, 51, 56
Equipment, managing, 59
Estate planning, 61
Estate plans, 35
Estate taxes, 41
Ethics, 26
Evolutionary change, 21, 28, 48–49
Experience, 57

Facilities, managing, 59, 62
Family, taking care of, 30, 31
Family beliefs, 13
Family branches, 53
Family business adaptability, 3
Family Business Advisor, 1, 61
Family business endurance, 1, 2
Family businesses, characteristics of, 9, 13
Family businesses versus public companies and change, 15
Family business retreat, 69
Family Business Values: How to Assure a Legacy of Continuity and Success, 21–22
Family council meetings, 74
Family culture, 13–14

Family goals, 60
Family leaders, 17
Family managers, 12
Family members, 12, 13, 36, 39, 43, 45, 50, 54, 55, 61, 62, 66, 68, 70, 73–75
  in the business, 33, 59–60, 76
  not active in the business, 14, 74, 80
Family ownership group, 25
Family relationships, maintaining harmonious, 54
Family size, change in, 61
Family tradition, 15. See also Traditions
Family values, 14. See also Values
  discussing, 76
Fathers, 26, 27, 69, 80
Fears, 40–41
Feedback, 55, 57
Finance, attitude toward, 61–64
Financial objectives, 25
Financial resources, 62, 64
Financial risk, 30, 31
Financial security, 15, 42–43
  for senior generation, 78
Financial strategy, 64
Financing paradigms, 62, 63
Financing Transitions: Managing Capital and Liquidity in the Family Business, 64
Flexibility, 6
Founders, 41, 68
Fourth generation, 50, 53, 54, 61, 64, 76
Frieda's, Inc., 16
Futures, imagining alternative, 48

Generations, responsibilities of, 79
Global marketplace, 5
"Golden Rule," 26
Granddad, 44, 46, 70
Grand Rapids, MI, 1

Growth strategies, funding, 63
Guilt, 71

Harvard Business School, 19
Heirs, 71
Heroic founders, 13, 42, 44, 51, 69
Hero worship, 13
Highlights Creed, 27
Highlights for Children, 27
Highlights for Children, Inc., 27, 33
History, place in, 41, 42
Honesdale, PA, 27
Honesty, 26

Ideas, new, 29, 46, 51, 69, 76
  adopting, 21
  conveying, 55
  generating, 64
  introduction, 46–47
  source of, 36
  stagnation of, 30
Incapacitation, 33
Incumbent CEOs, ideal, 67, 69
Incumbent CEOs, role in preparing
  for next-generation change,
  67–71
Incumbent generation, 61
Industrial Age, 68
Industrial Revolution, 5
Industry consolidation, 5
Industry experts, 47
Industry innovations, recognizing,
  60
Industry share groups, 55
Industry shifts, 34
Inflation, 35
Information Age, 6, 68
Innovation, 6, 9, 10, 37
  encouraging, 44
Insulation, 17
Integrity, 22, 23, 26, 29
International expansion, 35
Internet, 28, 48

Interstate Telephone Company, 60
ITC Holding Company, 60

Job security, 2, 43

Knowledge, depreciation of, 6
Knowledge, outside, 78

Laird Norton Co., 37, 44
Lanier, Smith, 60–61
Lanier family, 60
Leaders, 51, 79–80
  of culture, 51, 57
  of decision making, 51
Leadership, 2, 3, 52–53
  behind-the-scenes, 51
  importance of replacing
    frequently, 11, 14, 39
  learning, 5, 19
  style, 68
Leader's model for creating change,
  51
Learning organization, 78, 79
Lifestyles, 60
Long-term view, 10
Los Angeles, CA, 16
Love, 11, 12, 14
Loyalty, 4, 11, 17, 22, 30, 46, 77
  transferring, 41

Management, new, 75, 77
Management practices, 12–13
Management structure, 75
Management team, 65
  senior, 24
Managers, 25, 64
Managing change, 7
Marketplace, 5
  spending time in, 76
Marriott Corporation, 62
MCI, 60
Middle management, developing, 64
Mindspring, 60

Mission statement, 16, 27
Model for change, 40–51, 73
Mottos, 29
Myers, Caroline Clark, 27
Myers, Dr. Garry Cleveland, 27
Myers, Garry Cleveland, 33
Myers, Garry Cleveland III, 27, 28
Myers, Mary, 33
Myers family, 27–28, 33

Needs, 50
    understanding, 40–44
New behaviors, 31
New business initiatives, earmarking
    funds for, 74
New Economy, 6, 68
New tradition, 16
New York Times, 49, 50
Next generation, 42, 68, 69, 75
Next-generation leader, 67
Neyer, Alphonse (Al), 24, 25
Neyer, David F., 25
Neyer, Donald, 25
Neyer, Gertrude, 25
Neyer, Joseph Sr., 24
Neyer, Raymond A., 25
Neyer, Thomas L. Sr., 25
Neyer, William L., 25
Neyer family, 24–27
No-debt tradition, 62
Non-family employees, 9, 12, 14,
    41, 44
Non-family executives, 2, 4, 14,
    43–44, 68, 69, 75, 78
    hiring, 43
    key executives, 14, 43, 45, 61, 68

Objectivity, 19
Opinion leader, 74
Organization, freezing and
    refreezing, 47
Organization, introducing change
    into, 46–48

Organizational climate, 29
Organizational flexibility and
    adaptability, 73
Organizational structure, 54
Organizational wisdom, 56
Organization strengths, 44
Original business, selling, 53
Outside directors, 53, 54, 55. See also
    Board of directors
Overhead, 64, 65
Owners, 9

Parents, 6, 11–12, 14, 42–43, 71, 80
    entrepreneurial, 55
Past
    demystifying, 44, 51
    ideals of, 29
    keeping strengths of, 29
    preserving best of, 39
    respect for, 21, 28
Past practices, 19, 23
    as inhibitors of change, 23
Paternalistic management style, 17
Patience, 54
Patricide, symbolic, 19
People, managing, 59
Philosophy, guiding, 27
Pittsburgh, PA, 42
Policies, 36, 37
Powertel, 60
Predecessors, honoring, 46
Problems, identifying, 47
Problem-solving task force, 47
Professionalizing management, 37
Professionalizing the business, 66
Professional management systems,
    16
Profit centers, 74
    managers, 76
Prohibition, 34
Pruning, 45
Psychological stresses, 41
Public companies, 15

Rate of change, 2, 67
Real estate development and management, 24
Rebellion, 14
Refreezing the organization, 46–47
"Reinterpreting Values for Contemporary Challenges," 30–31
Reinventing the business, 6
Resilience, 1
Resistance, facing, 56
Resources for change, managing, 59–66
Respect, 11, 42, 53, 57
    mutual, 26
Restructuring, 24–25
Retirement, 33
    mandatory age, 11
Return on investment, 64
Revolutionary change, 21, 28
Richards, Roy Jr., 11, 75
Risk, 41
    averseness, 17

Scenarios, as help in creating change, 48
Seattle, WA, 36
Self-confidence, 57
Self-esteem, 77
Self-knowledge, 55
Senior generation, 5, 36
    CEO, 67
    financial security for, 78
Shareholders, 15, 41, 43, 52, 64
    buying out, 45
    education, 64
Sibling rivalry, 14, 75
Siblings, 56, 71, 74–75
Sibling teams, 80
Simsak, Nathalie, 36, 44
Skill-building ideas, 3
S. Martinelli & Company, 34
Social purpose, business, 77

Solutions, 47
Sons, 14, 52, 68, 78
Southwire Corp., 11, 75
Spouse, 74
Stability, 49
Stagnation, 30
Status quo, disturbing, 47
Strategic experiments, 60
Strategic incrementalism, 49, 51
Strategic perspective, 62
Strategic planning, 27
Strategic renewal, 79
    rate of, 6
Strategic success, 6
Strategic think tank, 76
Strategies, business, 62, 74
Structure for change, 64–66
Successes, past, 11, 19
Success inertia, 17
Succession issues, 5
Successors, 4, 5, 7, 11, 12, 13–15, 29, 39, 40, 41–43, 46, 48, 49, 54, 55, 67, 68, 80
    anxieties, 55
    characteristics needed to make change happen, 50–56
    leaders, 81
Sulzberger, Arthur Ochs Jr., 50
Suppliers, 45

Task force, 71
Tax planning, 61
Taylor, Tim, 37
Team members, 44
Teamwork, 68
Technological change, 34
Tenure length, 15, 17
The Living Company: Habits for Survival in a Turbulent Business Environment, 21
Third generation, 64, 66
Total quality management program, 16

Tradition of change, 56
  creating, 73–78
Traditions, 20
  balancing with creativity, 79
  dark side of, 22–23
  defined, 22
  distinguishing from value, 24, 28
  entrenched, 17
  institutionalizing, 13
Training, 31
Transition, generational, 35
Transition crises, steps to prevent,
  67–71

Unemployment, 35
Unfreezing the organization, 46–47
USA Today, 49

Vacuum cleaners, 2
Values, 19, 30–31, 50
  core, 22, 24, 25, 26, 28, 37, 45,
    51, 61

defined, 21
distinguishing from tradition, 24,
  28
foundation of, 20, 21, 50
reinterpreting, 30–31, 79
as strength or weakness,
  22–23
willingness to change as part of,
  44
Van Dyne-Crotty, Inc., 46, 66
Venture capitalist, 60
Ventures, business, 61
Viewpoint, 13, 14
Vision, 3
  for the business, 71
  for the future, 69

West Point, GA, 60

Younger generation, 6, 36, 61

Zaleznik, Abraham, 19, 20

The Authors

Craig E. Aronoff is Co-founder, Principal Consultant, and Chairman of the Board of the Family Business Consulting Group, Inc.; Founder of the Cox Family Enterprise Center; and current Professor Emeritus at Kennesaw State University. He invented and implemented the membership-based, professional-service-provider-sponsored Family Business Forum, which has served as a model of family business education for universities world-wide.

John L. Ward is Co-founder of the Family Business Consulting Group, Inc. He is Clinical Professor at the Kellogg School of Management and teaches strategic management, business leadership, and family enterprise continuity.

FAMILY BUSINESS SUCCESSION
The Final Test of Greatness
Craig E. Aronoff
Stephen L. McClure
John L. Ward

$23.00
978-0-230-11100-4

FAMILY BUSINESS GOVERNANCE
Maximizing Family and Business Potential
Craig E. Aronoff
John L. Ward

$23.00
978-0-230-11106-6

MAKING SIBLING TEAMS WORK
The Next Generation
Craig E. Aronoff
Joseph H. Astrachan
Drew S. Mendoza
John L. Ward

$23.00
978-0-230-11108-0

Keeping the Family Business Healthy
JOHN L. WARD

$50.00
978-0-230-11121-9

Family Business by the Numbers
How Financial Statements Impact Your Business
Norbert E. Schwarz

$45.00
978-0-230-11123-3

"Each Family Business Leadership publication is packed cover-to-cover with expert guidance, solid information and ideas that work."

—Alan Campbell, CFO, Campbell Motel Properties, Inc., Brea,

"While each volume contains helpful 'solutions' to the issues it covers, it is the guidance on how to tackle the process of addressing the different issues, and the emphasis on the benefits which can stem from the process itself, which make the Family Business publications of unique value to everyone involved in a family business—not just the owners."

—David Grant, Director (retired), William Grant & Sons (distillers of Glenfiddich and other fine Scotch whiske